OTHER HELEN EXLEY GIFTBOOKS:
Thanks Dad!
Thank you Mum. For everything
Thank you Mom. For everything
To a very special Friend

Printed simultaneously in 2007 by Helen Exley Giftbooks in Great Britai
and Helen Exley Giftbooks LLC in the USA.

12 11 10 9 8 7

Illustrations © Emma Davis 2007
Pam Brown © Helen Exley Creative Ltd 2015
Copyright © Helen Exley Creative Ltd 2015

Printed in China
ISBN-13: 978-1-905130-73-3

Pictures by Emma Davis, from the Soul Happiness collection
Words by Pam Brown
Edited by Helen Exley

Helen Exley Giftbooks, 16 Chalk Hill, Watford, Herts WD19 4BG, UK
www.helenexleygiftbooks.com

Dear Kay,

Thank <u>you</u> <u>to</u> <u>a</u> <u>real</u> <u>friend</u>

BY PAM BROWN
PICTURES BY EMMA DAVIS

*Love
Gail*

A HELEN EXLEY GIFTBOOK

10/7/18

LOVED! NEEDED

You find yourself loved,
needed, misse

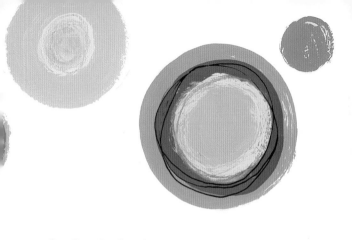

MISSED!

riendship is a sort of miracle.

SHARING A LIFE

Sharer of anxieties.

Sharer of silly jokes.

Sharer of excitements.

Thank you for everything.

HAPPY DAY

You know a silly postcard
on a Monday morning
brightens the day
– the heart. The Universe!

No need to

You seem to know my needs
and answer them long before
I've put them into words.

peak

YOUR

Medicines may be necessa

But your sm

SMILE

owers lift the heart.

the best restorative of all.

Feeling so

I am so very ordinar

good

hank you

for making me feel special.

LAUGHTER

The day started badly.
It was raining.
A fistful of bills.
A drift of circulars.
Gloom.
Doom.
But then you rang.
And made me laugh.

No friend has bee

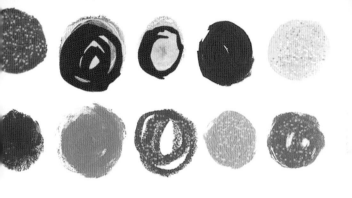

o constant.

No friend has been as true.
No friend has ever
meant as much as you.

MY GARDEN
IS BRIGHT
WITH PLANTS
THAT YOU
HAVE GIVEN ME.

YOUR GIFTS

ARE NOT PRACTICAL AND SENSIBLE.

THEY ARE ALWAYS FAR MORE.

THEY ARE GIFTS

OF IMAGINATION. THEY ARE

GIFTS OF DELIGHT.

ALWAYS THERE FOR ME

You are always there,
however distant,
constant as the Pole Star.
Unwavering in kindness
and concern – certainty
in an uncertain world.

You know
the words I need

You never say
what other people say.
You know the words
I need.

WE TWO

We don't need to ask each other.
We know the sort of play
the other likes, which books,
what music.
We know each other's most-loved
flower and scent. We know each
other's oddities. And so each meeting
is like coming home.

A MULTITUDE O

You have rescued me
so often – from hysterical spin driers,
jammed doors, burnt cakes,
missed trains, hopeless love affairs.
How could I have survived
without you?

MINI DISASTERS!!

You have solved
so many of my calamities –
bless you for your grin
and your incredible,
all enveloping competence.

RESPECT

Thanks for giving and expecting
respect – and for making me feel
very, very necessary.

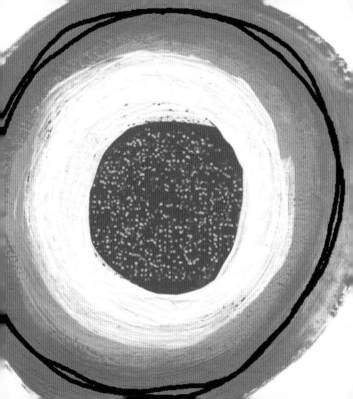

You give me
your time
– the most
generous gift
of all.

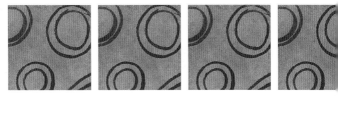

...knowing just whe

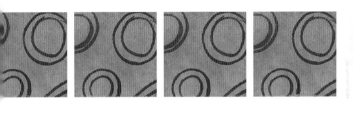

o be silent

Thank you for knowing
when to be silent.
When to sit and simply hold my hand.

QUIETLY AND CALMLY HELPING ME

Thank you for very quietly
and very efficiently
getting me out of what seemed
like an inextricable mess.

THE SMALL,
SILLY THINGS

It is not only the great kindnesses
that you have shown me – but
all the small and often silly things
that you have done to make me smile.
How dull life would
have been without you.

Small surprises – a bunch of
raggedy flowers on the doorstep
to start my day.
A fairy cake with a candle in the icing
on my birthday.
The book that I'd been searching for.
Fruit out of season. A ginger kitten.
– How did you know?

FREEDOM!

Thank you for
crazily outrageous days.
Which can encompass wicked
extravagances in fashion stores,
milk shakes by the sea,
gallery openings
and half-price sales.

TREATS

Friends carry a list in their heads:
clothes sizes, best-loved scents,
preferred shades, best-loved flowers
and edible delights.
And so find you Little Treats.

Every birthday,
every celebration, I can be certain
that at least one of my gifts
will be exactly what I hoped for.
The one from you.

LONELY

DAYS

You dropped in for a chat,
washed a few dishes, fed the cat.
Climbed those long stairs
up to the lonely flat.
You did these things for me
when I was in trouble,
eased fear and pain.
Thank you for that.

FRIENDSHIP
CAN MAKE
THE UNBEARABLE
BEARABLE.

Thank you
for making me laugh
when I'd almost forgotten
how to.

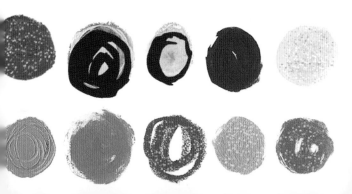

LAUGHING

TOGETHER

There is always
the endless traffic jam,
the closed café,
the deluge at the picnic,
the cancelled flight, the awful
meal we remember with a sigh,
a smile – a certain relish.
Friends can turn catastrophe
into happy memories.

ON MY SIDE

Thank you for telling me
　　what I already knew in my heart,
but calmly, clearly, positively.
　　　So that I could take
　　　　　it from there.

ONLY YOU WILL DO

There are times
when I have needed to tell someone
my fear, times when I have needed
someone to share a secret,
times when I have
needed someone to rejoice with me
over an achievement.
And those are the times when only
my friend will do.

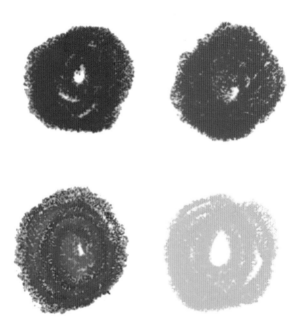

Thank you for being the best
sounding board in the world.
bring my half-baked plans to you,
my addled theories, muddled
resentments, shapeless dreams.
And come away with courage,
hope – and practicalities.

FRIEND:

Friends forgive. Mercifully.

When everyone else gives up
on me, you give a little sigh,
and set to untangling the mess
I've got myself into.

ORGIVE

THERE FOR ME

Other people are sympathetic,
concerned, kind –
but never there.
You are – whenever I most need you.

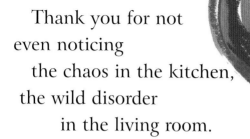

Thank you for not
even noticing
 the chaos in the kitchen,
the wild disorder
 in the living room.

BLIND TO ALL

MY FAULTS!

As we grow older
the times we retell our tales increases
– thank you for pretending
you've never heard them before.

SMILES & LAUGHTER

Here's a bouquet of smiles
and giggles
and helpless laughter,
of tears and sighs and whispered secrets,
of triumphs and disasters
we have shared.
With gratitude and love.

ALL OUR DAYS

…All the days we've walked
and talked together.
All the things we've shared,
our lives so interwoven that we can scarcely
think of life without each other.
Stay close – even if distance
should divide us.
I need your kindness and I need
your company.

...WHEN
I NEEDED YOU

Thank you
for dropping everything
and coming
when I most desperately
needed you.

There are times in life
    when we most need friends.
On standby.
    Ready to do anything
or go anywhere.
        Thank you for doing,
        being, just that.

Thank you for making me feel life

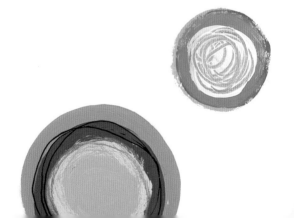

orth having – whatever happens.

SOUL MATES

We are all fundamentally alone
– but a few people have the knack
of diminishing that isolation –
of reaching out to touch us.
Thank you for being such
a human being – thank you
for your companionship.

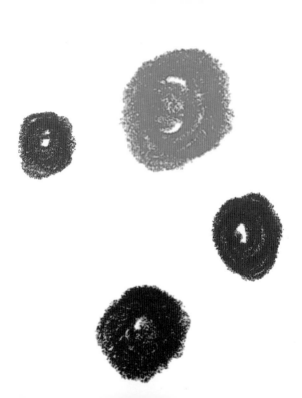

FOR A LIFE

How does one say thank you for a life?
I thank you for always being there when
I most needed you – in sickness and
in sorrow. In days of wild rejoicing.
But most of all, I thank you for being
who you are. Constant and kind.
Patient and forgiving.
Sharing my journey – the best of
all companions.

If you love this book...

...look out for other Helen Exley Giftbooks. There are over 300 thoughtful gift ideas listed on our website. There is something for mothers, daughters and other members of the family, and for friends. Here are just some of our other 'Friend' titles:

In Praise and Celebration of Friends
Words on Kindness
Words on the power of Friendship
To a very special Friend
Little things mean a lot
A Friend...

And a few of our other top books...

The Great Gift of Love
A Woman's Work is Never Done
Go Girl!
Taking Time to Just Be
Happy day!

Visit Helen Exley's website to see the full list of titles:
www.helenexleygiftbooks.com

What is a Helen Exley Giftbook?

Helen Exley Giftbooks cover the most powerful range
of all human relationships: love between couples, the
bonds within families and between friends.
No expense is spared in making sure that each book
is as thoughtful and meaningful a gift as it is possible
to create: good to give, good to receive.
You have the result in your hands. If you have loved
it – please tell others! There is no power on earth
like the word-of-mouth recommendation of friends.

Helen Exley Giftbooks
16 Chalk Hill, Watford, WD19 4BG, UK,
185 Main Street, Spencer, MA 01562, USA,
www.helenexleygiftbooks.com